THE AMERICAN NIGHTMARE

Black Women on Being Black in America

Compiled by
C. Nathaniel Brown

EXPECTED END

E x E

ENTERTAINMENT

Atlanta, GA

THE AMERICAN NIGHTMARE

Black Women on Being Black in America

CONTENTS

INTRODUCTION - C. NATHANIEL BROWN   1

1   DR. CHRISTIE M. PERSON   5

2   TELECIA STANTON   11

3   STACEY L. ANDERSON   17

4   TIKITA FICKLIN   29

5   DR. MONIQUE STONER   35

6   MONICA KAYE HARRIS   45

7   MAYA KING WILSON   53

8   MARY BAINES   59

9   NKEM DENCHUKWU   65

10   QUEEN NOLA   77

11   MICHELLE S. LOVETT   85

12   TRIBEL NICKERSON   95

     ABOUT THE COMPILER   101

This book is dedicated to Black women in America.

ACKNOWLEDGMENTS

Thank you to the amazing women who contributed to this project. Your stories and experiences, though many have been painful, have contributed to making the world a better place.

To my mother, Ellen Brown, thank you for being my first example of a strong, resilient Black woman. You taught me how to survive in a society that is not Black man friendly.

To my wife, Tarai, thank you for the 25-year start to our forever.

To my daughter, Brittnie, thank you for the words... I Love You!

To my late grandmother, Minnie Brown, and my late mother-in-law, Gloria Kemp, I hope I am making you proud.

To all my family, friends, and supporters, I appreciate each of you.

THE AMERICAN NIGHTMARE

INTRODUCTION

C. NATHANIEL BROWN

When I set out to provide a vehicle for a group of Black men, who were struggling with the current state of America, to express themselves, I heard from a few women who expressed their desire to contribute their voices and experiences to the movement. So, I created The American Nightmare: Women's Edition, Black women speaking on what being a Black woman is to them. They speak on racism, abuse of power, discrimination in the workplace and so much more.

Their stories inspire, motivate, encourage, and empower. They remind us of the pain they have experienced and the burdens they've had to bear. But we also see the resilience they possess to overcome any and all obstacles.

The impact of Black women in America can never be understated even though it hasn't been praised or appreciated enough. As you read this book, I hope their words forever change your life like they have changed mine.

So, as you begin this journey with them, this poem is my tribute to Black women.

Ode to You, Black Woman

There is nothing more beautiful than a Black woman! The vastness of her beauty can't be summed up by lines on a page, music in a song, or paint on a canvas. Her strength is that of mythical legend. She is the mother of our existence, the pillar of our family, and the backbone of our perseverance.

BLACK WOMEN ON BEING BLACK IN AMERICA

Because of you, Black woman, I am.
Because of you, Black woman, I am growing.
Because of you, Black woman, I am becoming.
Because of you, Black woman, I am a king.

I was blessed to be birthed by a phenomenal Black woman.
I was blessed to be raised by a group of powerful Black women.
I am blessed to be married to a beautiful Black woman.
I am blessed to be the father of a strong Black woman.
I am blessed to be connected to so many more extraordinary Black women.
I am blessed to admire you, Black woman.

On behalf of Black men, I salute you for being all that we could ever think we wanted or needed.
On behalf of Black men, I apologize for letting you down when we should have been lifting you up.
Many of us have not heard your cry, while others have ignored your pain behind your tears. Many have caused your tears. Many, like America, have let you down, put you down, and knocked you down.

But in the words of Queen Maya, I hear each of you say, "And still, I rise."
And you continue to rise…
And shine…
And soar…

THE AMERICAN NIGHTMARE

CHAPTER ONE

DR. CHRISTIE M. PERSON
MY JOURNEY AS A BLACK WOMAN
IN HEALTHCARE AND BEYOND

"Are you the doctor?" I've heard these words more often than I would like as I've entered an exam room in preparation for an eye evaluation. I'm an optometrist by trade, currently practicing eye care in an underserved community. I have worked in numerous settings where my professional status has been questioned because of my appearance. I'm young, Black, and female so I expect a little surprise from patients due to any one of the three factors. Yet, the connotation is always different when I walk into the exam room to see a Black or minority patient versus a white patient. There's a sense of pride and relief from fellow African Americans, while I'm sometimes met with disdain and confusion by those few Caucasian patients who can't mask their disappointment over seeing me instead of the white man they envisioned.

This is part of what it feels like to be black in America and a practicing healthcare professional. It's concerning that less than 5% of optometrists identify as African American. The representation is so poor because of the system that doesn't always display broader career options to African American students. When students make it into professional school, they are not always nurtured and given a place to flourish. There is often a constant struggle to fit into spaces that were not designed with them in mind. This is another reminder that disparities in healthcare exist because there aren't enough Black doctors for patients to relate to and for children to emulate.

When the white coat comes off, there is still a laundry list of stressors to face as a Black woman. There are a number of microaggressions, a term used to describe the common, but significant insensitivities committed against marginalized groups. It's the assumption that I must be part of the support staff when I tell white people I work in a hospital. The issue is not in being a part of the support staff, but in the assumption that I'm not in a position of leadership because of my race. It's the uncomfortable conversations when white people inquire about my natural hair. "It looks like ropes," was what one coworker said after I came to work with my hair freshly braided while in college. It's the private conversations that I'm not a part of when in predominantly white spaces. It's in certain stores when I'm observed more closely than the white customers. I've had more than one instance when I've been greeted less warmly than the white patrons in front of and behind me.

These daily interactions contribute to a number of internal struggles as well. They result in unfounded insecurities that cause me to doubt my ability because I know my white counterpart was likely afforded opportunities that I could never have imagined. These feelings of doubt manifest in the affirmations that I have to say some mornings because I know I must be prepared at a higher level than white individuals in my position. Additionally, these inward battles present as all the extra mental space that my thoughts inhabit because I'm a Black woman striving to thrive in a county that has not made provisions for me or my elders. This ugly truth is not far removed, particularly as I reflect on the fact that my maternal grandmother and grandfather's highest levels of education were third and sixth grade, respectively. They had to work three times as hard to acquire the land and home they lived in. This is just one more unnecessary source of pressure in the quest to make sure all of their hard work is not in vain.

In addition to the everyday pressures that exist, the safety of my loved ones remains at the forefront of my mind. I'm still afraid for my brother, cousins, and friends when they're out and about, knowing that their skin color is the first thing others see, instead of the amazing, caring men I know them to be. I worry for my 8-year-old daughter who cries some nights because she's afraid for her father's safety. It angers me that I have to discuss police brutality and racial profiling with a 3rd grader. These are conversations that I'm sure are not a regular occurrence in white households.

Not only is there concern for the men of my life, there's also anxiety for my own safety. Black women have been victims of unfair policing and racially motivated crimes for centuries. Our bodies have been violated, our lives taken, and our voices silenced. This is evident in the recent murders of numerous Black women from Sandra Bland to Breonna Taylor. Their stories are often not referenced with the same fervent call for justice as our Black brothers. These horrors are nothing new and date back to slavery, as well as the Jim Crow era. Black women are not immune to fear of the very ones who have vowed to protect and serve our communities. I, too, feel a sense of dread when I'm driving and see a police car in the lane behind me, knowing that my life and the lives of my loved ones could potentially be changed in an instant.

We are also expected to remain strong and emotionless while our families are ripped apart by racial injustice and systems rooted in hate and inequality. Thankfully, I grew up in a two-parent household. My home life was very stable and provided a place for me to grow without worry. Unfortunately, this is not every Black woman's reality. It saddens me to see the breakdown of the Black family and awakens a sense of awareness of the systems that are in place to keep Black men out of homes and in the penal system. Mass incarceration, economic inequality in Black neighborhoods, and failing school systems all contribute to Black men's absence. It is apparent in the lives of some of my family members and friends. As a result of this disparity, my chances of remarrying are lower because of the lack of compatible, eligible partners. I'm one of the blessed ones who can support myself financially, but there are many who have a different struggle. My ex-husband is very present in our daughter's life, but there are many who are raising children alone. It's not always due to the narrative that society would like us to believe. There are a large number of Black men who want to be involved in their children's lives but may be unable due to a system that has been rigged against them since the first slave ship landed on American soil.

I don't know what the future holds for race relations in America, but I do know that it's time to dismantle the current systems and to embrace a new way of relating to one another. It's time to change the way the world views Black women. We are not super-human. We are not without feelings. We need love. We need compassion. We need to be treated with dignity. We need to be understood. We need to be accepted just as we are. We need lasting change to take place. I'll know we're closer to progress when I walk into an exam room and receive the same amount of respect from each patient, regardless of their race. I'll know we're on the path to healing when my daughter no longer wonders if her dad and mom will make it home at night. We haven't arrived at that place, but I have to keep walking in faith and showing up for my loved ones every single day, hoping that one day that will be our story. It's what Black women do.

Dr. Christie M. Person is an author, optometrist, and entrepreneur. A graduate of Xavier University of Louisiana and Pennsylvania College of Optometry, she currently works at Grady Memorial Hospital in Atlanta. She enjoys reading, traveling domestically and abroad, as well as activities centered on physical fitness and a healthy lifestyle. She lives in Marietta, Georgia with her daughter, Laila.

CHAPTER TWO

TELECIA STANTON
BEING A BLACK WOMAN…
UNAPOLOGETICALLY

> *"Darkness cannot drive out darkness;*
> *only light can do that. Hate cannot*
> *drive out hate; only love can do that"* -
> *Dr. Martin Luther King, Jr.*

As I pondered over this topic, so many thoughts ran through my mind. It was not easy to grasp. Women wear many hats throughout life from being a mother, daughter, wife, and/or mentor. In the Black family, the matriarch is the one who sets the tone for teaching their children about love, family values, and equality. When we think of systemic racism, we tend to think about the discriminatory acts against Black men. As a Black woman, I was annihilated, scorned, and degraded by various races because they did not believe a little black girl with braided hair was deserving of private school education.

My father was killed when I was around four years old, and kids would criticize me because I was the product of a single-parent household. Kids and their families assumed we were poverty-stricken, but they did not understand that having a male in a household does not make it complete. My mom worked two jobs, and my granny taught me essential family values about loving people and treating everyone with respect. Growing up as a young child, I was not taught anything about racism, nor did the color one's skin matter to me, and I just wanted to play with other kids. I had white friends in school, therefore, I did not understand some of the concerns until years later. Individuals are not born hating another person; they are taught evil and hateful actions.

When I was 16 years old, I worked for a fast-food restaurant, and two white men called me a "nigger bitch". I remember feeling hurt, frustrated, and inundated. I knew I did nothing wrong and realized they were full of hate. As a Black teenager, I realized that I should not have to argue the validity of my existence in society and we do not share the same world.

> *"To bring about change, you must not*
> *be afraid to take the first step. We will*
> *fail when we fail to try."- Rosa Parks*

As a Black woman, I decided that it was time for me to educate myself and speak out on the changes needed in our society. I wanted to ensure that educating others, providing training, and ensuring racial discrimination will be a conversation no matter how uncomfortable it becomes. Black women are the pillar, the epitome of our society, whether we receive the recognition or not.

Being a Black woman is challenging because we are the glue that keeps the family together during trials and tribulations. We are willing to fight for our families and our beliefs no matter what obstacles we faced. We must take accountability for identifying who we are and establishing our destiny.

Being a Black woman is rewarding because we get to see our kings and queens raised in a structured home with values that were created by grounded ancestors who inculcated the strong abilities needed to survive.

I feel personal and generational exhaustion as I watch our people of color of all ages repeatedly being racially profiled, beaten, arrested without probable cause, and killed by the hands of the individuals who are supposed to serve and protect us. We are living in an unethical, discriminatory society that does not believe that systemic discrimination exists. It is disheartening that Black people have to prove their residence because some do not believe we belong in a particular neighborhood.

Although we cannot change everyone's way of thinking, we can peacefully protest, educate our children, and enact affirmative, realistic policies to our government. At times, we often feel powerless since racism influences our education system because they do not provide adequate funding for Black neighborhoods. We feel powerless due to socioeconomic statuses and the lack of business opportunities for Black people as we are delayed and denied business loans. The system is about power and maintaining control over us, but we must unite in order to combat police brutality and discrimination against our people of color.

According to the Merriam-Webster dictionary (2020), privilege is a special right, advantage, or immunity granted or available only to a particular person or group. For example, when a Black male and white male commit the same crime, and the court gives the Black male a life sentence, and the white male receives probation or a lesser charge. The system has allowed privileges for white people to survive for too long, and yet Black people helped build this country and do not have the same privileges.

As of today, there are more Black women in the marketplace holding high positions, leading generations on setting high goals, encouraging individuals to keep moving when faced with obstacles. We are competing for more jobs, managing corporate America, and using our voices to bring more awareness to racial disparities. We were underestimated and underrepresented because we did not reveal our talents due to self-esteem issues, stereotypes of being labeled "loud and ghetto", uneducated, non-marketable, lazy, and fear of rejection. Black women are not settling anymore, and we will not be made to feel invisible. We must stop being suffocated by the laws and unfair policing. We are exceeding expectations as we are running for political offices. We are police chiefs. We are senators. We are mayors. We are educators.

As I evolved, I realize that controlling my feelings allowed me not to be distracted by the hate in our society. I worked diligently as a single mother who proudly served and retired from the United States Army. I was truly blessed to accomplish my desired goals regardless of the contrary prejudice in our society. I did not allow anyone to destroy my vision and purpose. I feel that we can one day overcome some of the challenges we face, but we must take the first step and hold individuals accountable. If we stand for nothing, we will fall for anything. Remember, failure is not an option and never quit.

Telecia Stanton is the Founder of Dreamz2Success Movement, Inc., a non-profit organization that unites with the community through businesses, churches, schools, and families to help foster the development of character, life skills, and equip our youth to be leaders. From a young age, Telecia has helped people and ensured they receive adequate resources for success. As a mentor, she focuses on scaling down the walls of social disparities and determining solutions. Telecia is a disabled retired United States Army veteran who overcame many challenges in her personal and professional life. She holds a Master of Science in Business Administration, a Bachelor of Science in Human Resource Management, and an Associate of Science.

CHAPTER THREE

STACEY L. ANDERSON
FROM VIOLATION TO VIOLATION:
A CALL FOR HEALING IN THE AFRICAN
AMERICAN FAMILY AND COMMUNITY

If I were asked to choose a word that depicts the experience of African Americans, as a race since the days of slavery, I would choose *"molestation"*. Molestation, often a taboo and sadly, a huge family secret in the African American household, many think of molestation as an act of sexual assault. However, molestation is also the extent of harassing or pestering someone in an aggressive manner. The lingering and long-lasting effects of molestation, no matter the capacity can lead to strong emotions of vehemence and violation which produce feelings of breach, distrust, harm, damage, injury, trespass, transgression, assault, and defilement and begets stigma, anger, betrayal, and despair, to name a few. I would choose molestation as a word to describe the aggressive and harassing exploitation of African Americans who served controlling, forceful, authoritarian, and abusive white masters. Molestation could paint a harrowing picture of the aggressive whippings, beatings, bold harassment, and the cruel treatment of slaves. Molestation could attest to coerced sexual acts, mental and physical anguish that can never be fathomed. Molestation could indeed facilitate the truth of African American people who still continue to fight for freedom to live in another country where others are born free.

The aftereffect of brutal, ferocious, and savage acts of aggressive and harassing harm and injury, violation reciprocates into the African American family and community. Prevalent and passed down from generation to generation like a curse, this aftereffect leaves feelings of brokenness, robbery, loss of freedom, validation, innocence, choice, and opportunity. Violation is traumatic with symptoms of depression, despair, disrespect, fear, confusion, rage, and discord that unconsciously continue to evade the African American community. Traumatic experiences emulate behaviors that do not validate. Trauma does not affirm nor produce actions of love. More unfortunate, trauma causes guilt from aggressive actions that make others a recipient of that traumatic experience.

On April 14, 2016, my firstborn was murdered with a gun inside of a bar one of Pittsburgh's neighborhoods. Only 27 years old, he was shot three times and was found lying outside the bar with bullets to the head, back and shoulder by the time paramedics arrived. On the ground, he coded and was resuscitated. He succumbed to his wounds during surgery during the early morning of April 15, 2016. His murderer has not been apprehended and justice has not been served. It is every mother's nightmare to bury a child, but it is agonizing to conclude that someone's else's rage, discord, and discombobulation led to such a senseless and selfish act. It is an eerie and chilling feeling to ponder the extent another person's level of deep violation that could show no mercy or grace, placing self above God. Violation unleashed as an aggressive and harassing act inflicts tragedy upon parents, grandparents, siblings, children, and family members, of the deceased. Grief and loss change the perception of life and I have become a realist. I am a realist in the sense that life is precious, and death is inevitable, and that God grieves as

He comforts.

I share this story in essence of the enormous amount of times that I think about my son's murder and the minutes leading up to the bullets entering his body and wonder why he was the intended target. A young man of color, targeted by the police for infractions he was responsible for, and targeted because of his skin color. It is hard to accept that he was largely targeted and harassed by his African American male counterparts than white police officers. The generational curse of being mishandled and molested reared its' ugly head in the wake of my son's death. Someone else's feelings of pain, anger, loss of freedom, feelings of entitlement to respect and revenge ended his life prematurely.

Regrettably, molestation has been permitted to govern and destroy relationships in the African American community, both openly and privately. Molestation repeatedly consciously and unconsciously replicates what has been the experience as an African American. But why is this? There is a strange process of emulating what has been done. The beginning is pain and the end is pain. Suffering is pain. African Americans have experienced a great deal of suffering.

Pain is real and runs deep enough to make a person do profound things. The African American community has long hidden behind molested places that leave exposure and nakedness. Many African Americans have learned to mask the embarrassment of being molested in pain and being bound by molested pain. Pain has become a molested silence in the African American community. Yet, there is a desire to remain silent. Someone once said, "we are only as sick as the secrets we keep". African Americans have refrained for decades from being healed from this generational curse of being harassed and aggressively handled in so many ways that continue to make families and communities dysfunctional. The continuity of hiding behind the sick secret of molestation in so many different compartments is like a revolving door. Despite the open and infectious wounds that just ooze and seep, protection is no good if it is not self-protection. Self-protection is not fully healthy. There is a need to protect perpetrators who pose a threat and are not safe. Pain is a destroyer of self-esteem, self-worth, self-identity, and self-awareness. Pain hinders self-love and the ability to give love. Pain becomes the filter through which African American women relate to African American men, African American men relate to African American women, African American women relate to African American women, and African American men relate to African American men. African American children grow up and witness these broken relationships and the saga continues.

Women, molested as young girls, struggle through relationships and marriages looking for validation and acceptance. Men molested as young boys, struggle with self-identity, and/or keep silent and struggle to keep masculinity alive. Silence exists when protection is no longer a truth. Telling the story and enacting the hard parts, often brings shame, minimization, and blame.

No matter male or female, if you were to ask an African American for raw feelings immediately after being inappropriately touched or handled without consent sexually, certain words like dirty, nasty, and vile would be used. Words like dirty, nasty, and vile are destroyers of self-empathy. Yet, there is a common denominator. Validation is the common denominator. Validation indicates that someone or something is legally and officially acceptable. Validation is the antidote of every healthy relationship. Validation recognizes and affirms that people are important, valuable, acceptable, and worthwhile.

In all, validation is something that every human being desires, no matter the skin color. Validation is a priceless action and value. The very idea of believing and knowing that you matter, and you are accepted is most valuable. Validation breeds the courage and strength to birth dreams and desires. Validation removes any hesitation to share gifts, talents, strengths, ideas, and even weaknesses.

There are deep-seated, deep-rooted feelings of many African American men, women, and children after so many years of injustice, inequality, oppression, and discrimination from the hands of slave masters to the modern-day police officers. There is a need for acceptance. The fight to be free where everyone else is free molests African Americans on so many levels and there is a need for validation. Time and time, the need for validation appears, and sometimes it is given and sometimes it is not. Still, the consistent need for validation never diminishes. And just when the African American race conquers one or two controversies to mend and amend racial tension, even to the smallest extent, there is still a divide in a divided community with people who look the same as in a divided community with those who do not look the same. African Americans still fight to secure equality for acceptance in voting, employment opportunities, justice, and housing opportunities.

Molestation, the act of harassing, pestering, stereotyping, prejudice, assault, and even death causes illness in the heart and mind, therefore, there must be a place of validation and re-affirmation of individual and collective worth as a race. The healing process begins within *our own* African American community. Healing begins when every African American genuinely agrees to affirm, love, and care for the entire African American community and work together to form a united front with ammunition that can be used in today's America to dispel ammunition to rise above white police officers who only see skin color and death. Ammunition for preventing being counted out as minorities. Ammunition that places African Americans above the stereotypical ideologies where a higher price is paid for the consequences of pain, injury, and affliction. Ammunition that discerns between color blind and promotes color brave. Ammunition that removes the severe punishable reactions to unjust suffering and pain.

Recent protests around the country are sounding a need to be heard and live in harmony. African Americans have once again declared war on the injustices imposed and are weeping loudly for those painful places where African Americans continue to be touched and handled inappropriately. African Americans have again found a voice to demand a stop to such vilifying acts that are harmful, hateful, and bring death. African Americans are in demand to be free of situations and circumstances that are killing the African American race physically and mentally. Every African American must make an inner vow to never be silenced. The generations to come are depending on what is said and done today.

As a woman who is proud to be a deaf African American, I share the pain of molestation and violation. I have experienced tragedy, trauma, oppression, discrimination, injustice, and inequality. The road has been long, and it has been extremely painful. After the death of my son, in my grief, I honestly began to believe that the world was a terrible place. For a while, I could find absolutely no recourse. One day, I thought long and hard about what I could do to honor my son's memory. And since then, I have learned to become passionate and sensitive to the plight of the African American race and add to the story of the African American ordeal. As I add my story to the story, I invite others to join in adding to the story that will continue until the African American race is no more. The story must continue to detail the good, the bad, and the ugly; explain the blots and blemishes, but more importantly, tell of the resilience, the unity, and the validation that keeps strong among a group considered a minority. The story must continue to highlight the "majority" of the minority.

The African American family needs restoration in a very big way. Every member of the African American family deserves restoration to a rightful position of unity, love, and validation. African American women are valued nurturers and cultivators of new beginnings, dreams, desires, and growth. African American women are role models for the younger generations of African American women and mothers to African American children. African American women are admired for their intelligence, brilliance, and creativity. The contributions of the African American woman extend far beyond the scope of family. The gifts, strengths, and talents of the African American woman can change the world. That is just the enormous amount of strength that the African American woman possesses.

African American men are valued as protectors and providers and fathers for African American children. African American men are husbands for African American women. African American men are sons for mothers and fathers. African American men have important roles as a sibling, uncle, and cousin. African American grandparents need African American men as grandsons to carry a piece of the family legacy. African American men deserve restoration to their rightful place as a leader, provider, partner, and companion to the African American home.

As an African American woman, I watch the quandary of my African American brothers who are husbands, fathers, uncles, grandfathers, friends, and such during these very perilous times. My compassion and love are more present than ever. Although I cannot identify with being an African American male, I realize how much we need them. Most importantly, I learn to listen with my heart and offer no judgment for the depths of the African American man's pain, anger, fear, and heartache. In fact, among the things that are happening in America on a rather frequent basis, vulnerability, and the fear of whether they will return home at the end of the day is something that rests heavily on the heart and minds of many African American men. I look for ways that I can rectify my behavior, attitude, and actions so that change can begin. My validation begins with affirming the worth of every single African American man and learning to forgive without making excuses and encouraging healing.

COVID-19 may be a global pandemic, but so is the fact that so many years later, after the freedom wars and the civil rights movement, there are far too many episodes and occurrences of being touched and handled inappropriately. As I write, I appeal to the African American woman, what are "you" willing to sacrifice to end this pandemic that has endured for too long? What are "you" willing to do as an African American woman to contribute bringing to a halt the elements that have touched you *and* the African American man in ways that destroy dreams, hopes, and desires? Better yet, what are *you* willing to lend towards the astounding amount of dysfunction that is contained within the present-day

African American family?

Dysfunctional families do not begin upon cohabitation, it is baggage brought to a new dwelling. Dysfunctional families often bypass the belief of dysfunctionality and ignore hints of dysfunction. This dysfunctional unit, if not healed, will unpack the same dysfunction on the new family. Dysfunctional families employ members who mask and operate to the best of individualistic abilities until the weight of unresolved emotions and unresolved issues come crumbling down. No longer able to mask, dysfunctional family members capitulate to issues. Drugs, broken hearts, promiscuity, secrets, insecurities, death, and spiritual confusion are at the helm. Violence, toxicity, and abuse become actions. Mental anguish is often undetected yet lingers.

As I close, I take note of things that we as African American women may make valiant efforts to change, I assert that we must change the lens by which we see ourselves. We must change the lens by which we view and judge the men in our lives, no matter the role they play. Yep, he may have broken your heart and left you feeling less than a two-dollar bill. He still deserves love, even if it is not yours. As hard as it may be, we all crave validation and acceptance. You may not know his story, nor his struggles, and your expectations of him may not be what he is yet able to master. We are wiser when we assume responsibility for the dysfunction we create and add to our children. We violate children, when we allow our pain to stand between children and their fathers' Children, are taught how to validate, accept, and love their fathers, despite our opinion of him. African American ladies, no matter where you stand, there is a power within you. Powerful are your words and actions, enough to validate, affirm, and destroy generational curses, and build up homes. If we will ever heal as a race, family unit, and community, we cannot do it apart from our African American men. It is impossible. We have done it far too long.

Stacey L. Anderson is a deaf African American female who has experienced oppression, injustice, and discrimination. She is an advocate for individuals with disabilities. The mother of four children, she lost her oldest son to a tragic murdered in 2016. Stacey also has two daughters, Tamaiya and Geniya, and a son, Geoffrey. She enjoys spending time with family, cooking, writing and ministry. Stacey holds a bachelor's degree in Africana Studies from the University of Pittsburgh, a master's degree in Ministry Leadership from Indiana Wesleyan Seminary and is nearing the end of her Ph.D. journey in Organizational Leadership at Indiana Wesleyan University.

CHAPTER FOUR

TIKITA FICKLIN
IS BEING BLACK A CRIME

Nothing could ever describe the pain of a mother who has carried her child for nine months, gone through the pains of labor, invested time, tears and sweat mentoring that child to become who they are, for the world to view that innocent child as a threat because of the color of his skin.

I am the mother of three Black sons and one Black daughter. My oldest son is out on his own and I constantly check in on him because of the hatred in the hearts of others toward people who look just like him. I have accepted that I cannot be everywhere with my children, but my prayers go with them and before them to keep them from dangers seen and unseen. I constantly wonder, *why does the world devalue us because of our skin color?* I am an educated Black professional woman, but am I still viewed as a threat because of my melanin skin?

It's a struggle being Black in a world that sees your color as a threat, while not understanding that a human being lies within. What does a mother tell her child when someone of a different race calls them out of their name, bullies them, and makes them feel worthless? How do you stop hate from forming in that child's heart because of the mistreatment that they have endured? How do you stop that child from viewing all white people the same as the ones spewing racist venom? As a unit, how can we trust law enforcement that has sworn to protect and serve, but instead abuses and kills people who looks just like me? Even though all police officers are not the same, who wants to take that chance to trust any? Will you protect me today, to hurt or kill me tomorrow? No one should ever have to wonder whether calling the police could be worse than the situation you need their assistance for. Many would rather suffer through an incident, so they can at least live to see another day.

The fear that runs through my body when my son doesn't answer his phone when I call or doesn't immediately text me back is unreal. Or when my man leaves over the road for work and misses my call, and then I hear on the news that another Black man was killed in the area that he was working. The anxiety my body feels is literally breath taking on its own. My heart pounds. My mind races. I pray, "Lord, please protect and cover them under the blood of Jesus." I have to constantly pull fear down out of the atmosphere, and up out of me, and remembering the Word of God that says He has not designed fear for me. So, as a coping mechanism, I put on uplifting music to praise my way through the fear.

Man, I wish I could form a nation of people who looks just like me, but even within that circle jealous and hate are real. So many times, we say "Black Lives Matter", but do Black lives really matter to us. The black-on-black crime is just as real as the hate that the racist white police officer gives towards us. So not only are the police stopping us from breathing, we are stopping ourselves from existing. Now is the time for us to rise up and stand together in unity. Let go of the hate or the set you claim and build the Black community to the best it can possible be. Let's make sure that every individual reaches his/her full potential.

It amazes me to see the envy that arises within Black families because one is more successful than the other, reliving the story of Cain and Abel. We would rather invest our money with those who see us as nothing than to invest in our own people. We'd rather build their finances and their communities while ours stay in ruins. It is kind of like the crab in a barrel mentality, one crab starts to climb out, and when he is just about to achieve freedom, another crab reaches up and pulls him back down. How many Black families today are separated due to the selfishness of the one that should have mended the family, but yet has torn the family apart by sowing discord? The hate people give is real, but why does hate have to be given and received within our own communities and families.

Not only do I warn my children to keep an eye on others of different races, but to keep an even closer eye on the one who calls you a friend. Sometimes, that very friend is the one holding the knife that stabs you the deepest, with their lies, words, and silent, yet deadly, motives. To have to watch your back everywhere you go is exhausting. In some cases, you're not even able to find peace within your own four walls because disloyalty can show up in those who pretend to love you, build you, and claim to have your best interest at heart.

So, how do I protect myself, my children, and those I love? I know prayer works, but sometimes I feel like fighting...fighting for the little Black girls and boys who have no voice, those kids with no guidance, who were abandoned by the ones who should love them. Then when they turn to the streets to search for "family", they are labeled as gang members or criminals. Where does it end, and where does the true unconditional love begin? Is being Black in America a crime? CERTAINLY NOT!

To every Black boy who feels you are unworthy of love or feel like what happened to you as a child defines who you are now, let me be the one to tell you, you are worth it. You are worth the love. You are worth the fight. You are worth the respect and you are worth life. Never sell yourself short by looking at yourself through the lens of others. You are a king in the making, so you must walk as such.

To every Black man who feels like life has dealt you a bad hand, just know you can get up from this place and live. It's nothing worse than being alive but not truly living. Be the warrior you were created to be. You are not a threat. You are not an animal. You are not who the world views you as. However, you must conduct yourselves in the appropriate manner. Never give anyone any reason to doubt you. Be the king you are, love God, love your family, and love others. We need you to rise up and lead this lost world.

Tikita Ficklin is a multi-talented gem from Macon, Georgia, and the mother of three sons and a daughter. She is an author, singer/songwriter and actress, who has performed in such stage plays as: *From the Pole to the Pulpit; Damnation;* and *The Hem of His Garment.* *Tikita is a* licensed professional counselor for the state of Georgia. She relies on her relationship with God to impact the lives of others. Tikita, who earned a master's degree in clinical mental health counseling, is working on her doctorate in marriage and family therapy. She plans to establish a shelter for homeless families who have experienced domestic violence and other traumas.

CHAPTER FIVE

DR. MONIQUE STONER
WORKING WHILE BLACK:
A BLACK WOMAN'S STRUGGLE WITH
AMBITION, AUTHENTICITY AND
ASSIMILATION

If the truth will set us free then it's time for me to be brutally honest. It's 2020 and the color of our skin is *still* a major barrier holding us back economically, socially, politically, and of course, professionally. Black women are among the top producers in corporate America, yet we're not acknowledged as high performing employees. Instead, we're recognized as the high performing Black employees. And what infuriates me the most is the unwillingness of white corporate leaders to admit what we all know is true.

Race in the job market and in the workplace matter, and anyone who says it doesn't is lying. If anyone says they don't notice color, or they don't "see" race, is telling a bald-faced lie. Race is something we all notice. People definitely noticed me as a Black woman working in predominately white corporate environments for most of my career. No matter what we say, at first glance we immediately notice a person's gender and race. That's the truth and we all have to admit it.

It's also true that for the past several decades, Black women have not been getting their fair share of job opportunities, promotions or accolades in the corporate world. Mainstream media does not spotlight the plights of Black professional women, but instead chooses to focus on the "overt" barriers that women of all races face in the workplace, such as the pay gap, the proverbial glass ceiling, and the inequities in male-dominated industries. Yet, for Black women, there are also "covert" barriers that we relentlessly fight to overcome related to how we look, sound, dress and carry ourselves.

In most organizations today, diversity and inclusion programs are merely a check-the-box activity. Personally, I'm tired of the one-size-fits-all approach which has never led to anything transformative when it comes to race and equality in the workplace. By now, corporate leaders should have moved beyond the melting pot theory where diverse employees in their organization all think, act and look the same. It's time to embrace and convert the differences among people into a mosaic where everyone has the opportunity to maximize their full potential as unique individuals.

Diversity and inclusion must be about understanding how to be mutually inclusive of the various cultures, ethnicities, and identities of all people. Corporate leaders must be courageous enough to steer away from like-mindedness through assimilating people's differences (melting pot) and move towards like-mindedness through honoring those differences (mosaic). This is what Black people have spent the last 55 years fighting, striving and praying for in the workplace.

Working While Black (WWB) is not just another tagline that we've created to get attention or to ask for preferential treatment. On the contrary, it's a sardonic description of racial profiling and the racial bias used against Black women (and men) who work in corporate America. It's a term that encompasses how we're treated differently, perceived negatively, and often evaluated unfairly. Working while being a Black woman is especially challenging because we're made to feel like we're hindering and self-sabotaging our own careers based on our ethnic features and characteristics, even when we've proven ourselves to be strong leaders and stellar performers.

For Black women, working in corporate America is emotionally and spiritually taxing because there is a professional double-standard at play. The double bind we face is far more precarious than that of white women. Even though white women may also struggle to reach the highest levels of leadership in corporations, they're still seen as likable and relatable by white men. While on the other hand, Black women have a difficult time catching a break in either area. If we're too vocal, we're seen as angry or difficult, and become unlikable. If we're too subservient, we're not viewed as leaders and ultimately not respected. If we're too ethnic, we're perceived as eccentric and we don't fit in.

As someone who has worked in executive leadership roles for two state government agencies, three healthcare organizations, and two of the nation's Big 4 accounting firms, my race and distinct ethnic style were not only noticed, they were covertly scrutinized and low-key constrained. At both Big 4 firms, my white peers could raise their voice and use profanity when they were "passionate" about their stance on a project, assignment, or other work-related issues. Yet, when I would display even the slightest bit of frustration or opposition, I was told to "keep it down," "stop intimidating people" or "speak in a more pleasant tone."

It's rare that we find ourselves in a professional setting where we're not overwhelmingly outnumbered by white women (or white people in general), yet we're still perceived as threatening. Although research shows that the vast majority of Black women are dedicated workers, committed, team players with a high-level of confidence and ambition, the perceptions remain the same. This is what's known as Implicit Bias and it's generated by unconscious beliefs, stereotypical opinions, and media driven attitudes towards Black people as a whole.

According to a McKinsey and Leanin.org study, Black women receive less support from our managers than white women. This translates into us being less likely to have bosses who promote our work contributions to others, help us navigate organizational politics, or socialize with us outside of work. We also lack the kind of meaningful mentoring and advocacy that is critical for getting ahead. Inevitably, this often leads to Black women being left out of the informal networks that would propel us forward in our careers.

Black women also experience workplace harassment more than any other ethnic group. We are typically held to a much higher standard than our white female and male peers, although we're presumed to be less qualified despite our credentials, work product or performance results. As I look back over my 28-year, arduous climb up the corporate ladder, I can clearly see why it's been such a struggle. I have always been ambitious, but I refused to assimilate at the expense of losing my authenticity.

Fitting in Without Selling Out

All women are under pressure to conform to dominant masculine behavior in the workplace. Black women, however, are also under pressure to conform to dominant white behavioral norms. I often felt pressured to change how I dressed, my hair style, and my way of speaking, and also to become more sociable and less "ethnic". However, I knew that the more I conformed to white cultural expectations, I would lose my sense of personal identity and authenticity.

As a Black woman, it has always been critically important for me to establish and maintain my own unique identity and style. I'm proud of who I am and where I've come from, and I strongly believe that my outward behavior should be consistent with my inner values and convictions. My sense of authenticity is essential to my emotional well-being, productivity, and professional satisfaction. Yet, the higher I climbed up the ladder, the more pressure I was under to conform to white workplace norms, making it difficult "to be myself" at work.

When I worked for one of the top national accounting firms, I was invited to a lunch meeting with three white male partners. At the time, I had only been with the firm for about five months. During our small talk, the conversation focused on college experiences and one of the partners asked me a question about dorm life. They were all surprised to learn that I've never lived in a college dorm because I was married and had a son by the time I went to college. I went on to share that I have lived on my own since I was 15. I became a mother at 16 and a wife by the age of 18. Subsequently, as a teen mom, I had to drop out of regular high school and attend night school in order to get my diploma, and then I went on to attend college.

The response probably would have been better if I had punched all three of them in the face. I have no doubt that they would have been able to handle being hit much better than hearing about my backstory. By the looks on their faces and the feedback that ensued, it was obvious that they were most concerned about my story putting a blemish on the prestigious brand of the firm.

The Big 4 are known for recruiting the best of the best and only the top talent with impeccable backgrounds get accepted into their elite club. Despite where I started, I had an impressive work history which made me an ideal leadership candidate and experienced hire. Nevertheless, I was sternly told "not" to share those personal details with anyone else in the firm because I would risk being viewed and treated differently. And there it was... from their mouths to God's ears.

Life is hard for most Black women even before we enter the workforce. Whether we're raised in the suburbs or the projects, whether we became mothers at 17 or 37, whether we went to college through a traditional or a non-traditional pathway, being different and having different experiences isn't new to us. I had to overcome many obstacles to get to where I am today and I'm not ashamed of any part of my life's journey. It's simply unfortunate that for me, and other Black women, we are forced to continually walk a tightrope between "fitting in" and feeling authentic in the corporate world.

One thing I know for sure is that the workplace will not be equal until Black women have the same peace of mind and freedom to be ourselves that white women have. I look forward to the day when we can just put our best foot forward and let our careers progress without the added stress of hidden agendas constantly tugging at the edges of our consciousness.

Black women have feminine hearts and emotions just like females in any other race, but no one seems to notice or care how deeply we're affected by racial injustices in the workplace. Every day we must go the extra mile to keep ourselves mentally, physically, emotionally, and spiritually balanced in the workplace. This is a heavy burden for us to bear in the place where we spend most of our time and expend the majority of our energy.

At the end of the day, we must accept that working while black means realizing that injustices still exist in the workplace without feeling defeated by the fact that the dynamics are so much larger than us. It means recognizing that your stress and fears in the workplace will be different than your white female colleagues. And it also means understanding that no matter how good you are, there will still be those who will see you as a Black woman first... and an exceptional employee second.

Unfortunately, for me and my beautiful Black sistahs, we still have a long way to go before the corporate melting pot fully transforms into a mosaic. Nevertheless, we can still fit in and stand out at the same time. And take it from me, you can also settle in without selling out. Our day is coming. But in the meantime, I encourage you to hold your head up high and don't let anyone stop you from being your best self in the workplace. Embrace your ethnicity, individuality, uniqueness, flair, style, passion, and blackness. Don't be afraid to be who you are because what you bring to the table of corporate America is extremely valuable. And that's nothing but the truth.

Dr. Monique Stoner is a Life & Business Coach, Corporate Trainer, Consultant and Motivational Speaker. She's a Licensed Professional Counselor and a former Pastor. Monique has a Doctorate Degree in Organizational Psychology, a Master's Degree in Clinical Psychology and an MBA. She's a former consulting leader with Deloitte & KPMG and the founder of EXCELerate U-niversity™. Monique works with individuals struggling to overcome emotional and mental barriers to success. She specializes in behavior change management, personal development and energy healing. She empowers women and men affected by trauma, abuse, discrimination and harassment experienced in relationships, families and the workplace.

THE AMERICAN NIGHTMARE

CHAPTER SIX

MONICA KAYE HARRIS
THE AWAKENING

Growing up in the early 1970s and being raised by my grandparents, who were originally from the south, I heard my share of stories of racism and heartache. Fast forward to the year 2020 and I feel like I have somehow been encapsulated by an unknown mothership and taken back in history. To witness an innocent young man being hunted down like an animal and then killed for no reason is heart wrenching. It's heart wrenching to witness the murders of our Black brothers and sisters by the hands of those hired to protect and serve, to witness hangings of our brothers that are being deemed as suicide (when we all know that if any one of our Black brothers or sisters is contemplating suicide, it definitely won't be by hanging themselves on a tree or outside resemblance. There is too much painful history in that!). To witness the extreme hatred towards Blacks simply based upon the color of our skin by others is almost too much to stomach. These things alone are enough to cause premature aging, gray hair and the need for Xanax, while constantly shouting the phrase, "I CAN'T BREATHE"!

But being a Black woman during all of this has caused me to dig deeper into my faith and spiritual walk. It has been an awakening in all aspects that, even during the middle of this COVID-19 pandemic, has given me strength from deep in my soul. It's difficult being a Black woman and I call it a quadruple threat. Why?

1. I am a woman
2. I am a BLACK woman

3. I am fighting to gain respect and love from other sisters
4. I am fighting for the love, respect and honor from our Black men

In corporate America, you are automatically discriminated against if you are a woman, but to be a Black woman with a voice and intelligence makes you more of a threat to others. I'm not talking about a physical threat, but a powerful threat. As a Black woman, you must work twice as hard as your Caucasian female counterpart. You must dot every "i" and cross every "t". There is no room for error as your consequences are much more severe than those of your colleagues. And let's not even talk about being in a leadership position over a Caucasian male. Now, you are dealing with another level of discrimination. When you add hidden racism, it's like going into a concentration camp every day.

Nothing, and I do mean nothing, comes easy for a Black woman, at least not this one. So, I developed the following positive affirmations to help me get through the daily struggles of life:

- Never expect to be rewarded by man, but be grateful when it does happen.
- Remember our ultimate rewards come from above.
- When working, be mindful that you are working for God and not man.

- Always put your best foot forward and strive for excellence because you never know who may be watching.

It's difficult enough to have to go through life fighting for your right as a Black woman, but when other Black women aren't supportive, always competitive instead of collaborating, or harbor envy and jealousy towards other sisters, it makes it even more difficult trying to reach goals or develop leadership and opportunities within the community.

My desire is for Black women to realize who and whose we are. We are the mothers of the earth. We are the most powerful beings on this planet. We have let society poison our minds with hatred towards one another based on the complexion of our beautiful black skin. Dark-skinned Black women don't like light-skinned Black women or vice versa. Her hair is longer than yours, you don't like her. Her hair is straighter than yours, you don't like her. Her financial status is different than yours because she went to college, got a degree and worked hard towards her career goal, you don't like her. News flash! We are her!

All of us Black women, no matter skin complexion, body type, level of education, financial status, etc., are all the same. We are powerful queens that must tap into our inner ability to recognize that God made us different for a reason. But together we are unstoppable. Let us love on one another, support one another and move on to develop a legacy for our heirs that will be happy to call us mother. When you see another Black queen, greet her, embrace her, pray with her and grow with her. Together we can change the world and perhaps the people in it, beginning with our own brothers and sisters.

When it comes to our men, let me first say that I am in no way man bashing. However, there are a fair share of brothers out there who are just downright disrespectful, unfaithful, indecisive, and lacking the qualities of being capable of taking lead. God knows I've had my share. What we, as Black women, must realize is we must take a stand, change our views and make a difference. I believe that we women can change men. Uh oh! I hear a whole lot of murmuring and grumbling regarding that statement. Let me break it down for you. I am going to refer to the paragraph above about recognizing who we are as Black women. Once we realize our worth, no longer will we allow men to disrespect us nor will we disrespect ourselves. We will no longer be the side piece, side chick or whatever new terminology they have created for it. We will no longer dress scantily clad to gain attention, but our appearance and stance when we walk into a room will demand the right attention. No longer will we call ourselves the B-word or allow men to refer to us in such a manner. No longer will we be a booty call or give husband benefits to a man who doesn't think enough of us to change our last name. Enough is enough!

Society has also played a role in minimizing the role of the Black man by offering him lower wages and therefore many women have salaries that supersedes that of the man, which in turn has caused her to feel as though she is the breadwinner, the head of the household and can take care of all household essentials even without the income of the man. Therefore, she is quick to say those famous words, "I don't need a man. I can do it all by myself." That is a lie from the pit of hell. A woman's financial status does not replace the value of having a man in the household. If this were not true, God would not have stated that it is not good that man (nor woman) should be alone. He said, "let me make him a helpmeet," not a helpmate, but meet...one comparable/compatible with him. Together, they can help to meet each other's needs while working towards His purpose for the marriage. That woman's liberation stuff and modern-day slavery called welfare system destroyed the Black family. It took the Black men out of the home and gave assistance to the mother and children yet stated they could not remain together as a unit without losing the assistance they needed to maintain a household. This is why it is so important for us as a race to get back to the foundation of it all. We should keep God first, focus on marriage, create and maintain the family structure, grow and harvest our own, continue to build our own resources and support one another. Now that we realize who we are and our roles as queens, let us get back to building up our Black kings and taking back our respect. If we do this, I guarantee we will begin to see positive results and changes not only with our Black men but within our entire race.

Our Black men have a lot of stress. They need us to speak life into them. When husbands come home, they want peace. After fighting everything they have to encounter outside of their homes, they want to be greeted with peace, love and understanding when they come through that door. If there is someone in your life who doesn't appreciate that coming from you (man or woman) then maybe that person isn't the one you need to be with. Ask yourself, "Was this who God picked for me or is this my own selfish pick?" It makes a difference when we wait on God. Ask me how I know, and I will definitely tell you the cons of picking your own. I made that mistake and that's why I'm waiting and praying for my next one. Many times, we pick who we want and find out they're the wrong ones and then we pray for God to help us out of the relationship. Unfortunately, that's the wrong way. If we pray and seek God first, then He will give us who has specifically been designed for us and His purpose. Marriage is not about self- gratification only, but it is about serving a Godly purpose along the way.

Lastly, we women must deal with the anxiety of the safety of our Black men when they walk out of the door daily. We fear that our fathers, sons, brothers, uncles, cousins, nephews, and husbands will encounter the evilness of being racially profiled when they leave. We pray for their safety and the humble submission to our Father that they will return to us intact. The fact that for us single women, the supply of our Black men is limited, I cringe at the fact that they are murdering our future. They are murdering the future of forming a relationship and getting back to the foundation of marriage and creating a family. They are murdering the future of our Black men procreating with us (Black women) to create little black children who could one day become scientists, presidents, authors, and leaders. They are murdering more than the physical body; they are murdering our entire Black race. There has never been a more crucial time for us to band together as a race. We MATTER! Yes, this truly is the year of the awakening.

Monica Kaye Harris is CEO and Founder of My Scars Ministry, which helps individuals regain their self-esteem and identity after being wounded and scarred mentally, physically, emotionally, or spiritually. An ordained pastor and nationally certified chaplain, Pastor Harris serves on numerous organizations as a coach and mentor. She has received many recognitions for commitment to people, including community, ministry, and education awards. In addition to her ministry work, she enjoys writing, being a print model and acting.

CHAPTER SEVEN

MAYA KING WILSON
I WILL NOT REST

Growing up in 1990 with a white mother in an urban city was privileged in a way. I never thought of it like that at the time, but now I can see it was. We lived in a home with two parents. We had two or three Christmases depending on who was and wasn't getting along at the time. At the least, I would say it was much different than my friends' experiences. My light skin and white mother gave me a privileged lens.

Let me tell you the little I know about my parents' "love story". My father and mother met in high school. He was one of the only African American people in my mother's whole school. While I'm sure a few other families reacted poorly, my maternal family wouldn't stand for this relationship. My biological father being with my mother was apparently the straw that broke the camel's back.

In the late 80s, my parents married, enlisted in the military and were stationed together in Germany. My mother's family had disowned her by then. The first form of indirect or silent racism I ever knew was in my own family.

Fast forward to the 90s, my mother and father separated and eventually divorced. My mother married her second husband, who adopted my brother and me. He was a biracial man, much lighter than my biological father, but still was not totally accepted. They went on to have two more children that are also biracial but to outsiders present as white.

My stepfather used to laugh and tell us a story about a Ku Klux Klan album my grandparents played during one of his first visits to meet them.

One family discussion that sticks out to me was about our complexion differences within my immediate family. We told my younger sister, "We're all Black", and she responded by saying, "No, I'm not. I'm white." My brother and I replied, "You're Black. Look at your dad and us, we are Black!" My youngest sister burst into tears. She was upset about being called Black. I couldn't understand then what I understand now.

My maternal grandmother was the sweetest and most lovable woman you could ever meet. She told me a story about being confronted as being a Black woman because her skin tanned during the summer. She was told to sit in the back of the bus. That experience stayed with her. My grandmother, whom I loved so much and I know loved me, once told me there was a time she believed that stripes should be with stripes and spots with spots. What she meant was that Blacks with Blacks and whites with whites. She is the reason I believe in change.

My mother, by no real fault of her own, was not equipped to teach us to love ourselves and our culture. Her idea of education on our history and culture was making us watch Roots annually. We went to private schools until my 6th grade year. The demographics, as I recall, were pretty diverse. School is where I found a true cultural education and diversity amongst my friends. In high school, I joined the African American history debate team, where I truly began to embrace my journey as a Black woman.

If someone were to ask me now what I am, I would proudly and simply say Black. Why? Because for so long, I had been forced (in a way) to suppress my blackness since I was a part of a white family. Back then, if you were to ask me what I was I would specifically say biracial because I did not want to disappoint my family.

I got used to talking, dressing and composing myself in a proper manner to ensure I was never "ghetto" around my family. In a conversation I had recently with my brother, he called it code-switching. For those who don't know, it's like having a customer service voice and different voices for other settings and scenarios. I was trying to navigate two diverse worlds and trying to maintain the approval of my extended family, and it wasn't easy. There is always a love that comes with familial relationships, but their lack of speaking on our differences never helped me to feel accepted.

My appreciation and pride for my culture has developed as I immersed myself into the current state of injustice and inequality in the world, specifically America. Allowing myself to accept all of who I am and what makes me this person has made me open my eyes to my own ingrained prejudices and reevaluate my life perspectives. I have never had to change myself to be accepted in the Black and Brown communities the way I felt pressured to do so among my own white family. I would flat iron my hair and dress a certain way all for the acceptance of my mother's family.

It bothers me that people think being silent about

things like race and politics is a healthy way forward. It is not. As a person who grew up in a family that rarely talked about race or politics, I think it only buries the truths necessary to move forward. A misconception I have often heard is that mixed people get a pass on experiencing racism. This is also not true!

The last few months, I have spent time on the streets observing and protesting the injustices of Black and Brown people. I started out hoping to see that in 2020 there is less hate, less racism and less tolerance to the inequalities we witness daily here in America as a people of color.

Standing on the corners of my neighborhood saying Black Lives Matter has gotten me called racist slurs and followed home, where my children sleep. The experience of exercising my first amendment rights and telling the world that Black lives matter has been met with homegrown terrorists threatening to run our group over and kill us for what we believe is common sense... BLACK LIVES MATTER!

What have I learned, you may ask? I have learned that Black women are the least protected species on this planet and I'm going to change that! I have learned that no matter how hard I tried to ignore and deny its existence, racism is here and I'm afraid it never left. All I can say is that the American "dream" everyone is aiming for is a real nightmare for most, including myself recently. This land is stolen and built on the backs of Black and Brown people. I will not rest until there is equality.

Maya King Wilson is a community activist and mother of four children. She has a passion for the disenfranchised and seeing people achieve their full potential. The Pittsburgh native and Tampa resident is the product of a white mother and a Black father. In her spare time, she enjoys spending time with family and friends.

CHAPTER EIGHT

MARY BAINES
GOING BACK TO HEAL FORWARD

Did you know that Generational Trauma or Post Traumatic Slave Syndrome is a real thing? The mere thought of it almost seems unfathomable. Most of us have it and don't even realize it. Generational Trauma is passed down through genes. Is it possible that Black people are still dealing with unresolved trauma from our ancestors? Trauma can often lead to depression and anxiety as well as adaptive behavioral patterns. From slavery, sadism and the division of the family unit, to medical experimentation, police brutality, systematic oppression and more, it is fair to say that as a people we have had a brutal past, one that leaves most of us to question who we really are and how do we deal with the emotional trauma? Our culture has been stripped away causing us to unlearn and relearn mostly everything we've been taught.

I was born in November 1981. I didn't grow up playing with dolls that looked like me. Often teased because of my larger nose and full lips, I didn't start to love and appreciate my looks until my late 20s. We weren't taught that our skin tone, features, or that our hair was beautiful. Many days growing up, I wished I had lighter skin, a smaller nose, thinner lips and straight hair. I detested the word "nappy" that described my hair type and welcomed my first relaxer or "perm" that I received as a child to supposedly make my hair more manageable.

Aside from sideways glances and things whispered that I wasn't supposed to hear, my first real experience with racism happened when I was 12. I was living with my grandmother at the time in one of the first historically

Black neighborhoods of New Castle, Del., named Buttonwood. New Castle just so happens to be one of the places the Underground Railroad went through. Back in the 1940s, our family moved into the small four-street community that also housed the historical school Buttonwood School where my grandmother used to serve lunch. She used to tell me all the time not to go in the neighborhood next door called Collins Park. The community was predominantly white and she warned me that there were racist people that lived there and she didn't want anything to happen to me. I always found it funny that in the back of our neighborhood, past the railroad tracks, Collins Park was on one side and Buttonwood was on the other. The only entrance on that street was separated by concrete barricades.

One day, curiosity got the best of me. I had to see what the fuss was about, so I walked over there. I walked through the whole community, getting a few weird stares from residents. As I was leaving, I remembered thinking, *that wasn't too bad,* and couldn't wait to tell my grandmother that things had changed...or so I thought.

The next thing I know, I hear a vehicle coming fast down the street. I look back to see a huge black monster truck with huge wheels coming towards me. My eyes widened as I realized that the white man behind the wheel is in fact chasing me. He even came on the sidewalk revving his engine and I ran as fast as my legs could carry me. I was completely terrified and will never forget the look he gave me as he finally went past. The look screamed, "Get out! You don't belong here."

Another experience I remember is working in the restaurant area at BJ's Wholesale Club in New Castle. Because the store was understaffed, I was working the area by myself. The line at the counter was long. I was doing my best to get everyone's order correct. I noticed an older white man in line getting impatient and overheard him talking to the white woman next to him. He said, "This is taking forever!"

I took that moment to let everyone know that I was doing my best and would get everyone serviced as quickly as possible. I thought I was actually doing pretty well multitasking, putting wings and pizzas in the oven, and taking payments. Apparently, he didn't agree. As I wiped away sweat that was pouring down my face with my arm, I said to him, "Sir, I apologize if you feel I am taking long, but I am the only one here and I am doing the best that I can."

I guess he didn't like what I said because I heard him mutter, "These damn niggers always got an excuse."

I was shocked. As I walked toward him, I looked him in the eyes and asked, "What did you say?"

"You heard me!" he said with a satisfied grin on his face.

Let me first say that this wasn't one of my finer moments. I let the frustration of my day and his words get the best of me and before I knew it, I was giving him a piece of my mind! The words that came next from us both went by in a blur. Before I knew it, he tossed his soda at me. As it splattered all over my chest, I really went off on him walking around the counter and getting in his face. It didn't take long for management to come running up and of course, I was the one to blame.

No more than 10 minutes later, I'm outside waiting for the public transit bus, they had let me go. I didn't know back then to not let people get under my skin. Sometimes, I think back about my grandmother and all of the horrible things she dealt with growing up. Every morning, we would have breakfast together and from time to time, she would share a little bit about her past. One thing I'll always remember is her telling me how she felt when her dad, who was part Irish, was called a nigger lover when the family would be out in public. My great grandfather's skin was so fair that he passed for white and was able to use the white restrooms and water fountains. Her eyes would be filled with sadness and I remember being mad that she was made to feel this way.

While her children were growing up, most of her time was spent working for what she called "private family". Although they treated her well, she hated that she spent so much time away from her own family.

There have been other instances that I could go on for days. I'm sure each and every one of us can share an experience or two.

I often wonder about how things really were for our ancestors dealing with and experiencing things I couldn't even imagine. Besides stories I've been told by my grandmother, I realized I really knew nothing besides what the his-tory books told us. Over time, I realized there was a lot left out. Was that intentional?

My quest for knowledge led me to seek informational and educational material like the well-known documentary series called *Hidden Colors*. In the documentary, scholars and historians discussed how things were deliberately hidden about our past. I wasn't shocked to learn that Aboriginal Australian were Black with large noses and blonde hair.

The documentary helped me to realize that returning

to our culture and creating a sense of identity is something we must do to not continue the cycle of trauma.

I must say that I am proud to be a Black woman in America. We are a strong and resilient people. Our people have been through so much. This country was built on the backs of our ancestors. It is our time to make them proud and stand united because divided, we fall. Let's create more Black Wallstreets! We must lead the change we want to see.

Mary Baines is co-owner of Righteous Remodeling & Construction LLC with her husband Andre, and has been a general manager for self-storage facilities for the past eight years. She enjoys acting, singing and writing. Mary also enjoys being a Whole Food Educator and a loctician, taking special care of her client's natural hair journey. Documentaries and metaphysical topics are her favorite pastimes as well as listening to conscious music. Raised in New Castle, Del., Mary resides in Druid Hills, Ga., and is expanding her acting and music careers.

CHAPTER NINE

NKEM DENCHUKWU
COMING TO AMERICA

Emily Dickson once wrote, "Hope is the thing with feathers that perches in the soul, and sings the tune without words, and never stops all." I am that kinda 'girl' with unwavering faith and hope, no matter what comes my way. This is not about Eddie Murphy's journey, but about my journey in America that I hope will empower you. My experiences tried to break me, but the grace of God was sufficient, and I survived. I was born and built to survive, just like you. My faith is renewed with each sunrise.

We live in a world of uncertainties. To not become a shadow of our ignorance, foolishness, hopelessness, or fear, we must find ways to live our best lives, and not allow anyone to make us feel unworthy. Your integrity should be priceless. My integrity is my everything. Therefore, it is priceless.

I am unapologetically authentic, as much as I am unapologetically proud to be a Black woman. Therefore, there is no limit to what I can accomplish by the grace of God and doing my best.

Being a Black woman of Igbo decent is what I am and not what I am trying to be. I will not allow that to be devalued because someone has an issue with my Blackness and womanhood. It is inhumane to be discriminated against because I am a Black woman in a country in which I live and call home. When you are Black, you are discriminated for being Black. When your Black skin is very dark, they say, "You are too Black. You are too African!" When you are half Black and half another race, they say, "You are not Black enough." Ah ah! Wetin naa? (Ah! What?) Being African American or African is what we are, not what we are trying to be.

I was born on July 4 and raised in Southeastern Nigeria. My father died when I was 12, and my mother, an orphan, became a single mother of seven at the age of 38. By the way, my father was the Igwe (king) of my hometown. He married four wives and had 28 children. Before I came to America at 22, I had this wild, beautiful vision of the country, and couldn't wait to be a part of the "American dream". When my eldest sister mysteriously died at 34, leaving three babies behind, I was broken in many ways. So, leaving Nigeria for America seemed to be the best escape. While in the Bay Area of California, I lived with three of my siblings.

Living in America smelt and felt different...the weather, the air, the food, and the people, especially the people. It was/is a struggle trying to survive living here as an immigrant. Some days, we struggled to survive, but God blessed each day.

My first year in America was interesting! A group of students made fun of my accent. At first, I was flushed, but remembered whose daughter I am. I was confused because Americans also had/have accents but were ignorant to realize that we all have accents. Having an accent makes us unique. If I had low self-esteem, I'd have become a shadow of myself due to the bullies' constant caricature of my uniqueness. Eventually, many of them found my "not American" accent and the sound of my voice, alluring.

Fast forward to when I was job hunting in the healthcare industry since I have a Master of Health Administration (MHA). It was a discouraging time for me. I knew I was qualified to do the jobs I was applying for. The hiring managers knew, too. A white woman in her 30s said to me, "With your skills and in the process of obtaining your CPHQ (Certified Professional in Healthcare Quality certification), you are a threat to my job. Listen, you seem perfect for this job, but I am still trying to get my MHA. I'm sorry." The expression on her face was firm and sincere. I was hurt and felt so empty. I got educated to be discriminated for being educated? I silently questioned myself.

Another interview at a different organization with a group of Black women was more shocking. It's interesting how Black people hate on Black people, and then, complain when others hate on us. That morning before my interview, I felt like a million dollars because I was looking like a CEO. When I walked into the interview room, two of the three beautiful Black women sized me up, and mocked my having great qualifications and skills, yet unemployed? Meanwhile, the initial hiring manager, a white female, had guaranteed me the job based on merits, and even showed me my cubicle to start work on Monday. My joy was instantly shattered by my fellow Black women.

When I couldn't get a job with any healthcare establishment, I looked for work at Domino's Pizza, but was told I was overqualified. I was then advised by friends to reach out to Nigerian employers. Seeking opportunities with "my people" was somewhat hopeful. Rather than being given a chance based on merits, these predator-employers offered me a managerial position, but with a stipulation to become their mistress. It was an easy decision for me to make. I walked away with my integrity intact.

When adults bully, what do they teach children to become? I was once cyber-bullied by a group of older Nigerian men whose sexual advances I turned down. They used a fictitious email account to e-blast to many people, superimposed video and photo images of me in compromising positions. Less than a year later, the perpetrators were revealed to me, unbeknownst to them to date. Oops! Now, they will know. I felt sorry for them because they are miserable old men and should have been wiser. Otherwise, why would any happy person want to defame an innocent person's character? Go figure!

Let's talk about sexual harassment/abuse because they happen to many people daily, regardless of age, race, class, and sex. Can you imagine how many people have been abused in domestic violent environments or situations, especially during COVID-19? Heartbreaking! I remember the first time I was almost raped by a friend I trusted. I was in my 20s. Thankfully, two Oakland police officers saved me, and made sure I got home safely. There was that time I ended up in the ER after being brutally attacked for refusing sex with him. I also remember the second time I as almost raped. This time, it was in

Houston, by another familiar, but married man. I was 36. The grace of God found me, and I also fought like my life depended on it, because it did. All the men were Black.

Being a 'single' woman does not make me lonely, weak, vulnerable, desperate, or a sexual object to be devoured. There's more to me than being a woman, and Black. See me, don't judge me. But, if you see and still choose to judge me, especially for being Black and a woman, na your wahala be dat that! (That's your problem!) I am unapologetically authentic, and thankful for who God has made me to be.

It's okay to hate a behavior, but not okay to hate another or yourself. For you to hate another race, the burden lies solely on you because you are carrying a bag full of jealousy and inadequacies, and you lack self-love. So, when you want to hug hate, put yourself in their shoes, and choose love.

IT'S INTERESTING HOW WE HATE OTHERS, AND THEN, COMPLAIN WHEN OTHERS HATE US

I've met more than a handful of haters from different races. People hate because they want and choose to. No one is born a racist, a murder, a liar, a thief, a bully, a rapist... But, many of us were born to be artists. Many wonder how I went from obtaining a bachelor's degree in computer networking and a MHA to becoming a creative writer and a filmmaker. Though I do not use paints and brushes to bring images to life, I use words to paint relevant stories and information. Words do really speak! Sometimes, they become motion pictures. Words can mold or break us. The choice is ours, and I always chose positivity.

When I couldn't get a job in my industry as a healthcare professional, I was motivated by Iyke Obasi to write a book. In 2012, I wrote Tribal Echoes, and since then have 12 books under my belt, and won my first literary award, "Reader's Choice Award" in 2019 by the Houston Library Foundation. I really love writing inspirational books for the younger generations. Between 2014 and 2020, five of my creative verses were published in Oprah Magazine. As a bona fide filmmaker, I have produced 13 independent films, was once featured in Forbes (Digital Edition), and received Canada International Film Festival "Rising Award" in 2014.

I also experienced sexual harassments in the film world. As a Black woman living in America, I am constantly reminded that I am an African. My focus remains to produce good films, and do my best to stand firm in what I believe in, educate, inspire, and empower many female actors and producers (especially) not to succumb to sexual advances just to get ahead. A film project that I pre-produced was taken away from me because I refused to have sex with the executive producer. I was disappointed at first because I invested my time and skills, but glad I had my integrity intact.

Discrimination knows no boundaries. Many years ago, one of my babies was racially profiled at age 5, where most of our neighbors were white and racist. After constantly being bullied, I refused to raise my children in such a toxic space! As soon as my one-year lease expired, we moved to a 'cleaner' neighborhood with neighbors that cared for neighbors. "Love thy neighbor as thy self."

When a woman, especially a Black woman, is single, it does not make her desperate, available, or angry. After being married for a while, I became single by choice. Sometimes, some relationships are not meant to be or last. It can be a challenge being a parent, and I know many parents can attest to this fact. But, I do love the challenge because I am blessed with four amazing children, and I do my best for them. It can be a struggle sometimes to provide certain things, but God always blesses the day. So, when someone thinks that I am not enough to be valued because I am no longer Mrs. Somebody, I question their common sense and childhood orientation. You see, I live in a beautiful, secure neighborhood, and some Black people have issues with it because they maybe jealous, and battle with their inadequacies. They ask how a single, Black woman with four children is always happy, and able to afford to live in an upscale neighborhood, and then, inadvertently refer to me as an "Ashawo" (a prostitute). Wow! They turn blind eyes to the glaring fact that I am a hardworking mother, favored by grace. By the way, nobody is always happy. Not even God is always happy. Some men, if not most, tend to talk down on or about a woman, especially when they are intimidated by her, lack self-esteem, or when their manhood is in question.

A long while ago, a white guy called me a ho. I returned the favor, and he blurted out, "Bitch! You are just an angry Black woman." I felt sorry for him and relayed a Bible verse, which made him angrier. He called me a ho because he wanted me to be the first Black female to sleep with him, like it would have been a privilege for me to have sex with a white man. Na wa o! (Wow!) He tried to belittle a woman who anchors her strength on God. But he failed. The keyword here is "tried". Nobody has the power to steal your joy or downgrade your integrity unless you give them that power and the key to your wholeness.

I do not understand why anyone would believe that they are better than others because of the color of their skin, class, experiences, or gender. The same red blood runs in us, and when we die, our hearts stop beating. We are all equal. When we make room for hate, it becomes a big part of us, for as long as we nurture it. It is refreshing, rejuvenating, rewarding, and absolutely the best experience when we choose kindness because love knows no color.

For me, being a woman is beautiful. But, being a beautiful Black woman living in America is truly an experience, the kind that has the power to make you question yourself, all that you are and hope to be, break you, or mold you to becoming the best of you. The choice is always ours to make.

My experiences included times I was depressed, caused by grief especially. Depression is real! It's okay to say that you are depressed. There's nothing shameful about it. Your life could be saved when you talk about it. When I was grieving in 2019, I expressed to a few people that I was depressed. They scolded me not to say it aloud because it was "an abominable expression". I was shocked because they are educated and supposedly enlightened. I eventually broke the yolk of depression by accepting and talking about my feelings, being prayerful and thankful, making positive things and the people that love me my escape, and remained hopeful.

As a mother, I work very hard to make sure my children are mentally, emotionally, physically, and spiritually nurtured. They are proud Nigerian Americans. I remind them to stay rooted to all that make them strong, and to be the best of themselves. I pray they will not experience more racism, and if/when they do, I pray they anchor their strengths and fears on God and all that their father and I continue to teach them.

Every human being has the capacity to persevere, change, and become the best version of themselves.

After 26 years of living in the "land of opportunity", I am still working hard to get my feet wet and my head above water. However, as long as I breathe and can catch my breaths in between my helter-skelter, I have hope in my dreams, and I will keep pushing.

If there's a next life, I pray to be a woman, a Black mother of Black sons and daughters, and unapologetically authentic. Today (not tomorrow) is my chance to be greater than who and what I was yesterday. Therefore, I unwrap each day with a smile and a thankful heart. What I do today matters, and what you do today matters because tomorrow is the future, and not guaranteed. Therefore, let love and kindness be the hallmark of your words and actions.

Nkem DenChukwu is an award-winning author, a film producer, a woman whose strength is anchored in God and being a mother of four. She also advocates for battered women, men, and children, and continues to promote awareness about mental illness and suicide prevention through written and spoken words. As a mother, Nkem teaches and reminds her children to always be proud of being black, Nigerian-Americans, and to stay rooted to all that makes them strong and unstoppable. Nkem earned a master's degree in Health Services Administration and a bachelor's degree in computer networking, but her first love is in the arts. She also enjoys gourmet cooking and photography.

THE AMERICAN NIGHTMARE

CHAPTER TEN

QUEEN NOLA
YOUR LIE, MY TRUTH:
BREAKING THE CYCLE

When you wake up in the morning in America, what thoughts cross your mind? Are your thoughts and emotions filled with anger, frustration, stress, anxiety, tears, pain, etc.? How have you been coping while constantly enduring so much trauma while seeking peace? Do you yearn for sympathy, compassion, love, or just nurturing friendships, relationships, and a strong support system?

If I told you that the majority of men and women in America are traumatized by one or more past and current situations, would you believe me? Living in America has its strengths and weaknesses, good and bad, as well as positive and negative qualities. Sometimes, it can seem like our lives are not our own. We have been lied to, deceived, traumatized, mind-controlled, battered, bruised, and even killed on numerous occasions for not just the color of our skin but also the intelligence of our minds.

When you look back and pay attention to the patterns in this country and how history always repeat itself, it's sad. They want you to pay attention to, lose focus on, and believe in what they want you to, instead of allowing you to have a free-thinking mindset. Think about how our parents, grandparents, and even great grandparents lived and survived all the havoc and trauma placed at their feet. Many had children and tried to maintain their household. This country has always put Black people's backs against the wall. There is always something else to overcome and survive.

I was furious for many, many years. I blamed my mother for so many things that happened to me without knowing she was repeating the cycle of what was done to her. I never thought I could break the chain that had so much power over me. But one day, I chose to totally detox my mind, body, and spirit. I had to unlearn a lot of information that was taught to me and seek answers for myself. I chose not to walk around angry, bitter, mean, and revengeful because of what I had endured throughout my life. I craved peace and I was going to have it.

A lot of Black people are drained, overworked, stressed out, irritable, angry, and frustrated from constant mistreatment in this country. We have always had to work extra hard for anything we accomplished or created. I watched my mother work multiple jobs to make ends meet. Where there were hardworking families and close knitted communities, there was always some enticing vice put in place to aid them into spending unnecessarily, pumping money back into rich people's pockets.

As a Black woman living in America, I have endured more than my share of trauma and pain brought on by childhood molestation, child abuse, family violence, and more. I watched my mother be oppressed by the system via social, health and human services. My mother worked so many hours doing a variety of jobs and gigs that she was not able to be home to take the time to raise, protect, and educate my siblings and me. In all honesty, I believe she did what she thought was best in her mindset. My mother had a rough life that left her scarred and mentally ill. What she witnessed as the norm in her upbringing, repeated onto her children.

As I watched my mother growing up, I knew what I did not want for my children. I said they will never know what it felt like to have utilities turned off, not have enough food on the table, not be able to discuss how they felt, be forced to keep secrets that should be told, be nurtured and loved at home so they won't have to be desperate for it somewhere else, not have the responsibility of an adult as a child or teenager, learn valuable ways to grow and develop at a young age to position themselves on the path of their purpose sooner rather than later.

The trauma and pain I experienced as a child and teenager almost ruined my life. I went through 12 years of counseling and therapy. It, along with my faith, changed my life and gave me another chance at becoming the best version of myself. Our past can hold us back if we do not have a strong foundation to stand on or be mentally, emotionally, and spiritually at peace on our journey. Living in America can take a toll on all of that. There is so much hate and anger in our faces every single day as a reminder of our skin color and oppressions so many are enduring.

How can one move forward consistently when there are so many reminders and history lessons everywhere you turn? Among them are: the riots; commercials; social media ads; videos; protests; and actions taken by police against Black people. There is so much tension in the country and world which is keeping so many from even starting the healing process. Depression, PTSD, and suicides are on the rise with so many not knowing how to cope. There is more than enough going on in America that makes it harder for anyone to move forward.

Going long periods of time without a solution or treatment plan will eventually lead to some sort of chaos. Seek help without being ashamed. It may not be easy but after what we have all endured during the pandemic, know you are not alone. With so much happening, it can weigh on our mental and overtake us completely. Do not allow the enemy or past situations, traumas, and tragedies to rob you of your present or future. Many hold on to their past as if it is a security blanket not knowing what it could cost them or how it might destroy or put a dent in God's plan for us.

In order to grow, we must let some things go so that we can successfully move forward in our lives. Sometimes, it may appear easier said than done, but trust me, we must stand on God's word, feed our spirit, and strengthen our faith. I know firsthand what damage the past can cause. Take time to read, gain the knowledge and understanding, and develop coping mechanisms to enhance your lives. You will be able to encourage and empower others who are struggling, too. I pray healing and strength over the lives of those reading this to enable you to become better people, friends, mothers, fathers, employers, employees, sisters, brothers, husbands, wives, teachers, mentors, advocates, etc.

In life, we all will endure or experience trauma or tragedy at least once. How it affects us mentally, emotionally, physically, or spiritually depends on how we handle it. It is not about what you go through but how you choose to handle and come out of it. Some of us do not realize the strength we have inside. Instead, our weaknesses play a major role in the destruction or misdirection of our lives. Where we come from and what we have been through sometimes dictate the type of life we have. We do not have all the answers, so sometimes we require help from others to be able to move forward.

The world is full of people and life-changing situations. Our lives change dramatically after enduring some of the most traumatizing events. Under these circumstances, our emotions and actions get the best of us. Sometimes, we think and believe we have a handle on things by buying a big house, having kids, getting married, getting a good job or promotion, driving a fancy car, or living a luxurious lifestyle. But many people are stuck in marriages, relationships, jobs, and friendships, that have their minds and hearts in pain, sadness, frustration, anguish, and irritability. Many are so mindful of what the world thinks of them and wants them to look and be like that they start compounding their unhappiness. Understand and know that once you are not in the public eye, the mask comes off. There are very few people in this world who are happy and secure within themselves and will not be swayed or manipulated by anyone else's beliefs or opinions of them. They remain in their walk with God by focusing and meditating on His word. This leads to peace of mind, joy, and happiness.

Sometimes, doing what's right for you does not make you selfish or inconsiderate. I have learned that sacrificing myself and my happiness for the benefit of another person (who does not deserve it), is not the best judgment call in the long run, especially if your positive energy is being drained by someone else's negative energy. Do not just wake up but WAKE UP! Stop complaining and worrying about everyone else's faults, problems, business, and struggles if you have not first focused and corrected your own. Make sure your kitchen is spotless before you volunteer to help someone else clean theirs. In other words, "Mind and Handle Your Business." Then spread more positivity and love throughout your home, community, and job. Get involved in something you are passionate about to stimulate change. Together, we can make a bigger impact in society. You are more than the color of your skin. You are leaders, advocates, business owners, mothers, fathers, sisters, brothers, friends, neighbors, and the list goes on. When I first started writing, I was headed in a different direction, but I decided to encourage and uplift you. I hope I have done that. Keep pressing on, pushing through and moving forward. All of us have a story that is still being written. Use your voice and make a loud noise for positive change. Look around you and start there. Right in your own back yard. Your community needs you. Continued blessings my good people.

"We can't do it all, but we can all do something."- Queen Nola

Dianna Adams aka Queen Nola is an entrepreneur, motivational speaker, life and business coach. Originally from New Orleans, Queen Nola grew up in Natchez, Miss. The mother of three children, two with special needs, has a passion for cooking and helping people. She is founder of Caring Hands & Hearts Foundation, Inc., a nonprofit organization that advocates for families and individuals with disabilities and specials needs. She is owner of Queen Nola's Catering and Concessions, which also started a #Cooking4Causes initiative to shed light on the foundation's mission. In addition, Queen Nola launched Savory 7 Flavors seasoning and sauce line. She resides in Buford, Ga.

CHAPTER ELEVEN

MICHELLE S. LOVETT
SUDDENLY

The past year has been an example of what being a Black woman in America is. It has been a rollercoaster of emotions, life changes, certain hope, and the introduction of an uncertain future. But Black women are expected to be strong as usual, while fighting off all the stereotypes of who we are and what we do.

As a lupus survivor and as someone who, at birth, was given less than 48 hours to live, I know about being counted out, overlooked and undervalued. But I also know about resilience, fighting back and overcoming against all odds. That's what makes a Black woman's journey so unique...we deal with so much in our personal lives, in our communities and in the world that we experience the ups and downs but still come out winning when 'suddenly' happens.

Last year this time, I was well on my way in my acting career, hosting a radio show, and my personal and spiritual life were truly reaching another level. Some would define me as a serial entrepreneur because while wearing those hats, I managed to curate my first book project, which was an Amazon #1 bestseller in multiple categories, plus co-produced documentaries that are currently out on Amazon Prime. I was touring and receiving awards all over the globe, including a proclamation, participating in radio/tv interviews, and more.

Have your dreams ever become your reality? Have you ever had to adjust your way of living? 2019 will never be forgotten. Every time you looked up, I, and everyone attached to me, were winning. 2020 was starting out the same way. I co-hosted the Dr. Martin Luther King Jr. parade back in my hometown (Dade County, Fla.). I was invited to Superbowl, Grammy and Oscar functions, and private celebrity parties and events. I filmed different shows, including Volume 3 of "Life, Love & Lockup". Truly, things were moving and shaking, and I was living up to my name... MeMe All Over!

Suddenly, it all vanished.

I was in Las Vegas on vacation, relaxing, clearing my mind, resting my body, and preparing for what was supposed to be the continuation of this winning season. I could feel the success for the rest of 2020. Suddenly, across the TV screen, I saw breaking news about China having a serious virus outbreak called coronavirus disease (COVID-19). I must admit, at first, I didn't take the issue seriously. As the days went by, things began to get to me mentally and emotionally. I remember telling my friend that it smelled like a hospital in the casinos. You could tell things were beginning to quickly go left.

Out of precaution, we terminated our vacation early. Two weeks later in Atlanta, we had a book cover reveal for *Life, Love & Lockup, Volume 3: Appointed Angels*. Our guests normally support in large numbers, but many were uncertain about going out, so the event was intimate. As the days went by, more and more breaking news flashed across the TV & radio about the crisis. Suddenly, the number of COVID-19 cases (and the number of deaths) began to increase across the globe. Everyone was asked to quarantine, wear masks, stay six feet apart when in public and a curfew was implemented. Some businesses began closing early while others completely shut down. Grocery stores started running out of food and essential items. I found myself traveling miles out, hunting for food, water, and tissue. At times, I would go into Publix only to find empty shelves and freezers.

Once, the outbreak hit Albany, Ga., I knew we were in trouble. Most of my father's family lives there. The thought that I may never see them again caused my depression and anxiety to climb to an all-time high. At first, I wouldn't even go out the door. I was extremely horrified, plus, I believed the virus was in the air. However, the verdict is still out on that opinion.

The United States has had different outbreaks before but none like COVID-19. Hospitals and funeral homes started reaching capacity with bodies. Church, the place where most people laid burdens down, was forced to shut down. We were not prepared for anything of this magnitude. Things truly got out of hand. I asked God if he was punishing us because the world had become so wicked.

Things seemed like a nightmare to me. For example, I couldn't believe the President decided to administer lupus medication to COVID-19 patients. I'm glad the medication assisted some who were able to survive. However, I didn't agree with lupus patients having to go without their medicine due to a shortage because doctors were instructed to make COVID patients a priority instead of lupus patients. As a lupus survivor, that hurt my heart. I literally saw patients begging for their meds and was still was unable to get them. However, I'm thankful that in 2016, I started slowly coming off some meds while going cold turkey on others. I'm glad God had a plan for my life and led me to living a more holistic and natural remedy lifestyle. But even participating in a holistic way of life had its challenges. For example, shipping and receiving products took longer. There was even a shortage on natural products. Just like regular doctor visits, the holistic doctors started virtual visits.

But as strong Black women do, I adjusted. But thing continued to change in me and in society, as. I began worrying about the thought of never seeing my father again. My father and I both have underlying health conditions that make us susceptible to COVID-19. So, it wasn't safe for us to be around others, let alone each other. We also live in different states and flying is considered extremely risky for us at the time. I haven't seen my father since March. Typically, we don't go that long without seeing each other. My daily prayers include that God will heal and protect my dad and me. The thought of one of us contracting the virus, being hospitalized, and potentially dying alone truly haunts me. I try to hold on to the word of God and my faith because that's all anyone can do at this point.

At the same time we are dealing with a health pandemic, the country is experiencing unrest. The president spews racist and divisive remarks, protests erupt in the streets after a series of Black murders at the hands of police, millions of people lost their jobs during the shutdown, and the economy is suffering.

As a little girl, my parents would tell me stories about the racism they and their parents encountered. They told me to be thankful for living in the times we live in because I probably couldn't survive what they had to endure.

History class taught me about protesting/boycotting and the different individuals that fought, suffered, and died so that I would have access to different luxuries and privileges today such as the right to vote, dining in restaurants of my choosing, and shopping in stores I like. It's disheartening watching racism wake, shake up, and go live in 2020, and to see the covers pulled back where racism no longer resides in sheep's clothing.

It all reminded me of when the Black man was first brought to America. He wasn't even thought of as human. In fact, the United States Constitution only gave him ⅗ humanity. Therefore, he was more often treated inhumanely then human. Then came the emancipation proclamation, followed by the Civil Rights Act, the Fair Labor Act and many other laws and acts designed to help African Americans. Ask yourself...are we taking full advantage of the benefits at hand? Some are but surely far too many aren't. You must agree, when we consider the number of those incarcerated, those who are into drugs and crime and those who have become a part of the criminal justice system.

Dr. Martin Luther King Jr., Rosa Parks, Malcom X, Al

Sharpton, and Jesse Jackson, just to name a few, all assisted in paving the way for us all. During these unprecedented times, I've witnessed discrimination because the color of my skin and gender and I've seen innocent lives taken by police brutality. However, I've also seen people come together and take a stand. More minorities have started businesses and taken back what others have stolen from them. Now, people are screaming "Black Lives Matter!" Well, Black lives have always mattered.

Dr. King's speech, "A Knock at Midnight", comes to mind. He left behind various warnings of the challenges to come. He said we had some difficult days ahead. But he also told us, "Those who love peace must learn to organize as effectively as those who love war" because together we will stand but divided, we will fall.

Although some change has occurred over the years, it is imperative, now more than ever, that we all stay woke and remember how Christopher Columbus "discovered" America. Yes, the Emancipation Proclamation technically freed the slaves in 1863, but there are some who still want to treat African Americans as slaves. This country supposed to be the land of the free. But there are so many indicators and examples that clearly demonstrate that America isn't the land of the free for all. Our lives are in the hands of government officials who couldn't care less. This pandemic, coupled with the social unrest, have made us look at the world as we know it. Things have shifted and we must adapt. We must activate our faith, remain focused keep our eyes on the prize.

It's not always easy. There are many days I've had to encourage myself. Being single and quarantined have made me tap into places I did not know even existed. Many say things will get better, although sometimes it doesn't seem like it. I watch the news and see COVID-19 cases and deaths increasing across the country. I see more cases of police brutality and deaths of African Americans at the hands of police.

This can't be the new normal. That's why I will continue to uplift others, especially Black women because we are the heart and soul of this country. We have always made a difference and I know that we will create the change we want. I always say, we complete, not compete.

When we come together as a race and as a country, we witness change and we're going to witness it again. Like Dr. King and others in the past, I see leaders who won't accept how Black people are being treated. We can no longer choose between non-violence or violence but between non-violence or non-existence.

I trust in God and believe things will get better. Be encouraged because the breakthrough is coming. Lean not to your own understanding. God will see us through, I'm certain. Make no mistake about it, sooner or later it will all work in our favor. Help is on the way. We just have to hold on to God's unchanging hand. Suddenly, in a blink of an eye, things will turn around and get better. Maybe America just might finally be great, and we won't be judged by the color of our skin but by the content of our character.

Michelle S. Lovett is a bestselling author, publisher and self-proclaimed serial entrepreneur. She is curator of the *Life, Love & Lockup* series that includes three volumes of anthologies and documentaries. Founder and CEO of MeMe All Over LLC, Michelle is also a regular on the entertainment scene as an actor, a radio show host, and a producer. A lupus survivor, she is an advocate for other survivors and a mentor to women entrepreneurs. In her spare time, Michelle enjoys writing; traveling; and spending time with family and friends. She resides in Atlanta, GA.

THE AMERICAN NIGHTMARE

CHAPTER TWELVE

TRIBEL NICKERSON
OUR STORY IS NOT OVER

I am the middle of five children. When I was nine years old, I discovered that the man I thought was my father was not my father. My mother was always a hard-working woman and my stepfather raised me, but I didn't really feel like he loved me. He was extremely strict and stern, although he took care of me and provided food.

I was always a loner and a tomboy growing up. I think that contributed to my troubled childhood as I was molested by several family members for years but never shared it until now. At 15, I wanted to run away from home because I felt like nobody loved me. I told my mother I was leaving and never coming back. I started dating gangsters and drug dealers, who I knew were all wrong for me, but I loved the attention they gave me. I felt like they could protect me. I remember one guy pulled out a gun and put it to my head. I thought I was going to die. So, I started dating older men, looking for a father figure, looking for an escape from my reality.

At that time, I was also getting an understanding of how much women were objectified, and the amount of pressure placed on us to be everything for everybody. We almost always have to be perfect. I didn't know if I could live up to that or if anybody could live up to that.

As a Black woman, that pressure intensifies because of how others think and feel about us. As a Black teenager trying to deal with all the other chaos in my life, I was then introduced to how cruel racism was. Right after high school, I was hired by a white woman to clean shelves in a store. She handed me a bucket that had black, dirty water in it. I told her that the water was black and dirty. She replied, "You shouldn't have a problem putting your hand in it because you are black, too, right?"

I was shocked. The schools I attended in Virginia were racially mixed and I never had any experiences with racism before that.

When I went to college at 18, I met a wonderful man and we fell in love. I thought my life was finally taking a turn for the best. I remember yelling at my mother telling her that I was getting married and I would never need anybody ever again. I married him, we had a son, and he was a great provider and the best father, yet we still ended up divorced.

By the time I entered corporate America, I learned that other Black women had some of the same experiences of being abused, feeling the pressure to be perfect, and being mistreated because of their skin color.

Being a Black woman in corporate America comes with its fair share of challenges, including gender discrimination and workplace bias. I think 75% of Black women view themselves as ambitious towards our career goals with 25% hoping to reach management or leadership positions. I had a difficult time in the workplace dealing with men because they would come on to me sexually and if I didn't entertain them, they would treat me differently. It truly bothered me how many men assumed that just because I'm friendly, outgoing and an alpha female that I wanted sex. Even though I suffered sexual harassment and sexual assault in the workplace, I never reported anything.

I suffered in silence for years because I didn't want that to add to the pressure I was already feeling being one of the only Black women in most of the business settings and having to fight 100 times harder than anyone else in the room. I've never fully healed from some of those experiences.

One day, a white man told me that Black women are assertive, angry, and have attitudes. I think Black women are tired of being disappointed in the workplace because we're overlooked and underpaid, despite being highly qualified and dedicated. How others see us effects how they treat us. I have been passed over for promotions several times in favor of less experienced and less qualified white co-workers. In one company, a white woman, whom I trained, was promoted over me when clearly, I had more work experience and seniority there.

In the workplace, men are generally regarded as natural leaders and women must overcome serious challenges to be recognized as competent, capable leaders. Add minority women to the mix and the challenges multiply significantly. We've suffered through so much abuse, mistreatment, sexism, racism, pay disparities and so much more. For so long, we've felt that we weren't in a position to speak up for fear of losing our jobs and being 'blackballed' in our fields.

I felt I needed to be strong and suppress my emotions over the years. I felt like I was living for other people and not being myself. I was miserable and felt alone. I was in a dark place! And I know many of Black women who have experienced the same things and felt the same way.

I decided to get a mentor to help me figure out what was going on and what I needed to do to begin to live for me. I began reading self-help books and the bible to regain my faith and strength so I could take my life back and focus on me. I had to stop being a people pleaser and live my best life for me.

I now have several businesses and am proud of all I overcame to get to this point. But I have so much more I want to achieve both in business and in my personal life.

I know that other Black women feel the same. That's why there are so many who have started their own businesses and mentor other Black women to do the same. I started Ladies Empowered and Driven (L.E.A.D.), a women's empowerment organization to help women heal from all that we have experienced. I also created the Women of Honor Award Show in Atlanta to recognize women who have achieved success in various fields, including business, ministry, entertainment and more.

Our story is not over. My story is not over. As Black women, we still have a lot of work to do. But I realize it's a process. People often think I have it all together because of personal achievements, successful businesses and my work with celebrities over the years, but behind closed doors, I was miserable from the age of 14 until the age of 47. That's when I met my biological dad. I met him one time and I never saw him again. I needed to meet him to forgive him because I was still living with a void in my life.

Even with all the success stories we've had as Black

women, we still have some hidden issues we need to address and heal from. And we will. But in the meantime, we will continue to be strong mothers, wives, sisters, daughters, mentors, entrepreneurs, and friends...despite the obstacles in our way.

Tribel Nickerson is a mentor of young girls, an entrepreneur and a workshop and event host who loves to help build people and their businesses. She's the founder of L.E.A.D., a women's empowerment organization. Tribel is heavily involved in the media and entertainment industries. She serves as an executive board member with an Atlanta film festival and a director. The Portsmouth, Va., native is the mother of two adult children, who enjoys cooking, shopping, traveling with family, and playing the base guitar in her spare time. She resides in Atlanta.

ABOUT THE COMPILER

C. Nathaniel Brown is an award-winning writer, filmmaker, publisher and writing coach. A multiple bestselling author of 17 books, he is founder and CEO of Expected End Entertainment, a full-service media and entertainment company based in Atlanta. The company's mission is to entertain, educate and empower through various services that include film, television, book publishing and writer coaching to name a few. The Baltimore native's personal mission is to help people dream bigger, live their dreams and impact their world. One of his goals is to help 10,000 writers to become published. He has also written, produced and/or directed more than 30 films and mentors up-and-coming actors, screenplay writers, producers and directors.

For more information about *The American Nightmare: Black Women on Being Black in America*, or *The American Nightmare: Black Men on being Black in America*, contact ExpectedEndEntertainment@gmail.com.

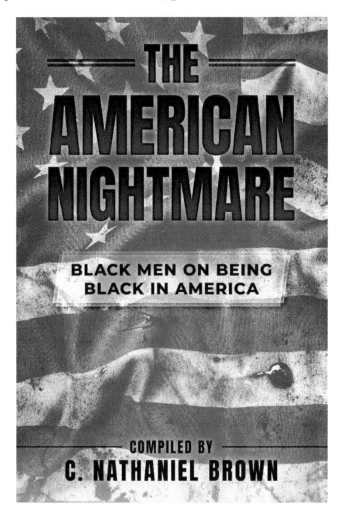

BLACK WOMEN ON BEING BLACK IN AMERICA

Made in the USA
Columbia, SC
12 September 2020

18668114R00061